HOWL

AND OTHER POEMS
BY
ALLEN GINSBERG

' Unscrew the locks from the doors !
Unscrew the doors themselves from their jambs !'

Martino Publishing
Mansfield Centre, CT
2014

Martino Publishing
P.O. Box 373,
Mansfield Centre, CT 06250 USA

ISBN   978-1-61427-819-1

© *2015 Martino Publishing*

Cover design by T. Matarazzo

Printed in the United States of America On 100% Acid-Free Paper

HOWL

AND OTHER POEMS

BY

ALLEN GINSBERG

' Unscrew the locks from the doors !
Unscrew the doors themselves from their jambs !'

THE POCKET POETS SERIES : Number Four
The City Lights Pocket Bookshop
San Francisco

*The Pocket Poets Series is published
by the City Lights Pocket Bookshop,
261 Columbus Avenue, San Francisco
11, and distributed nationally by the
Paper Editions Corporation.*

Manufactured in the United States of America

DEDICATION

To—

Jack Kerouac, new Buddha of American prose, who spit forth intelligence into eleven books written in half the number of years (1951-1956) — *On the Road, Visions of Neal, Dr Sax, Springtime Mary, The Subterraneans, San Francisco Blues, Some of the Dharma, Book of Dreams, Wake Up, Mexico City Blues,* and *Visions of Gerard* — creating a spontaneous bop prosody and original classic literature. Several phrases and the title of *Howl* are taken from him.

William Seward Burroughs, author of *Naked Lunch,* an endless novel which will drive everybody mad.

Neal Cassady, author of *The First Third,* an autobiography (1949) which enlightened Buddha.

All these books are published in Heaven.

— A. G.

CONTENTS

HOWL FOR CARL SOLOMON

When he was younger, and I was younger, I used to know Allen Ginsberg, a young poet living in Paterson, New Jersey, where he, son of a well-known poet, had been born and grew up. He was physically slight of build and mentally much disturbed by the life which he had encountered about him during those first years after the first world war as it was exhibited to him in and about New York City. He was always on the point of 'going away', where it didn't seem to matter; he disturbed me, I never thought he'd live to grow up and write a book of poems. His ability to survive, travel, and go on writing astonishes me. That he has gone on developing and perfecting his art is no less amazing to me.

Now he turns up fifteen or twenty years later with an arresting poem. Literally he has, from all the evidence, been through hell. On the way he met a man named Carl Solomon with whom he shared among the teeth and excrement of this life something that cannot be described but in the words he has used to describe it. It is a howl of defeat. Not defeat at all for he has gone through defeat as if it were an ordinary experience, a trivial experience. Everyone in this life is defeated but a man, if he be a man, is not defeated.

It is the poet, Allen Ginsberg, who has gone, in his own body, through the horrifying experiences described from life in these pages. The wonder of the thing is not that he has survived but that he, from the very depths, has found a fellow whom he can love, a love he celebrates without looking aside in these poems. Say what you will, he proves to us, in spite of the most debasing experiences that life can offer a man, the spirit of love survives to ennoble our lives if we have the wit and the courage and the faith — and the art! to persist.

It is the belief in the art of poetry that has gone hand in hand with this man into his Golgotha, from that charnel house, similar in every way, to that of the Jews in the past war. But this is in our own country, our own fondest purlieus. We are blind and live our blind lives out in blindness. Poets are damned but they are not blind, they see with the eyes of the angels. This poet sees through and all around the horrors he partakes of in the very intimate details of his poem. He avoids nothing but experiences it to the hilt. He contains it. Claims it as his own — and, we believe, laughs at it and has the time and affrontery to love a fellow of his choice and record that love in a well-made poem.

Hold back the edges of your gowns, Ladies, we are going through hell.

William Carlos Williams.

HOWL

for
Carl Solomon

I

I saw the best minds of my generation destroyed by madness, starving hysterical naked,

dragging themselves through the negro streets at dawn looking for an angry fix,

angelheaded hipsters burning for the ancient heavenly connection to the starry dynamo in the machinery of night,

who poverty and tatters and hollow-eyed and high sat up smoking in the supernatural darkness of cold-water flats floating across the tops of cities contemplating jazz,

who bared their brains to Heaven under the El and saw Mohammedan angels staggering on tenement roofs illuminated,

who passed through universities with radiant cool eyes hallucinating Arkansas and Blake-light tragedy among the scholars of war,

who were expelled from the academies for crazy & publishing obscene odes on the windows of the skull,

who cowered in unshaven rooms in underwear, burning their money in wastebaskets and listening to the Terror through the wall,

who got busted in their pubic beards returning through Laredo with a belt of marijuana for New York,

who ate fire in paint hotels or drank turpentine in Paradise Alley, death, or purgatoried their torsos night after night

with dreams, with drugs, with waking nightmares, alcohol and cock and endless balls,

incomparable blind streets of shuddering cloud and lightning in the mind leaping toward poles of Canada & Paterson,

illuminating all the motionless world of Time between,
Peyote solidities of halls, backyard green tree cemetery dawns,
wine drunkenness over the rooftops, storefront boroughs of
teahead joyride neon blinking traffic light, sun and moon
and tree vibrations in the roaring winter dusks of Brooklyn,
ashcan rantings and kind king light of mind,
who chained themselves to subways for the endless ride from Battery
to holy Bronx on benzedrine until the noise of wheels and
children brought them down shuddering mouth-wracked
and battered bleak of brain all drained of brilliance in the
drear light of Zoo,
who sank all night in submarine light of Bickford's floated out and
sat through the stale beer afternoon in desolate Fugazzi's,
listening to the crack of doom on the hydrogen jukebox,
who talked continuously seventy hours from park to pad to bar to
Bellevue to museum to the Brooklyn Bridge,
a lost battalion of platonic conversationalists jumping down the
stoops off fire escapes off windowsills off Empire State out
of the moon,
yacketayakking screaming vomiting whispering facts and memories
and anecdotes and eyeball kicks and shocks of hospitals and
jails and wars,
whole intellects disgorged in total recall for seven days and nights
with brilliant eyes, meat for the Synagogue cast on the
pavement,
who vanished into nowhere Zen New Jersey leaving a trail of
ambiguous picture postcards of Atlantic City Hall,
suffering Eastern sweats and Tangerian bone-grindings and
migraines of China under junk-withdrawal in Newark's
bleak furnished room,
who wandered around and around at midnight in the railroad yard
wondering where to go, and went, leaving no broken hearts,

who lit cigarettes in boxcars boxcars boxcars racketing through snow
toward lonesome farms in grandfather night,
who studied Plotinus Poe St. John of the Cross telepathy and bop
kaballa because the cosmos instinctively vibrated at their
feet in Kansas,
who loned it through the streets of Idaho seeking visionary indian
angels who were visionary indian angels,
who thought they were only mad when Baltimore gleamed in
supernatural ecstasy,
who jumped in limousines with the Chinaman of Oklahoma on the
impulse of winter midnight streetlight smalltown rain,
who lounged hungry and lonesome through Houston seeking jazz
or sex or soup, and followed the brilliant Spaniard to
converse about America and Eternity, a hopeless task, and so
took ship to Africa,
who disappeared into the volcanoes of Mexico leaving behind
nothing but the shadow of dungarees and the lava and ash
of poetry scattered in fireplace Chicago,
who reappeared on the West Coast investigating the F.B.I. in
beards and shorts with big pacifist eyes sexy in their dark
skin passing out incomprehensible leaflets,
who burned cigarette holes in their arms protesting the narcotic
tobacco haze of Capitalism,
who distributed Supercommunist pamphlets in Union Square
weeping and undressing while the sirens of Los Alamos
wailed them down, and wailed down Wall, and the Staten
Island ferry also wailed,
who broke down crying in white gymnasiums naked and
trembling before the machinery of other skeletons,
who bit detectives in the neck and shrieked with delight in
policecars for committing no crime but their own wild
cooking pederasty and intoxication,

who howled on their knees in the subway and were dragged off the
     roof waving genitals and manuscripts,

who let themselves be ...... in the ... by saintly motorcyclists,
     and screamed with joy,

who blew and were blown by those human seraphim, the sailors,
     caresses of Atlantic and Caribbean love,

who balled in the morning in the evenings in rosegardens and the
     grass of public parks and cemeteries scattering their semen
     freely to whomever come who may,

who hiccupped endlessly trying to giggle but wound up with a sob
     behind a partition in a Turkish Bath when the blonde &
     naked angel came to pierce them with a sword,

who lost their loveboys to the three old shrews of fate the one eyed
     shrew of the heterosexual dollar the one eyed shrew that
     winks out of the womb and the one eyed shrew that does
     nothing but sit on her ass and snip the intellectual golden
     threads of the craftsman's loom,

who copulated ecstatic and insatiate with a bottle of beer a
     sweetheart a package of cigarettes a candle and fell off the
     bed, and continued along the floor and down the hall and
     ended fainting on the wall with a vision of ultimate c...
     and come eluding the last gyzym of consciousness,

who sweetened the snatches of a million girls trembling in the
     sunset, and were red eyed in the morning but prepared to
     sweeten the snatch of the sunrise, flashing buttocks under
     barns and naked in the lake,

who went out whoring through Colorado in myriad stolen
     night-cars, N.C., secret hero of these poems, cocksman and
     Adonis of Denver — joy to the memory of his innumerable
     lays of girls in empty lots & diner backyards, moviehouses,
     rickety rows on mountaintops in caves or with gaunt
     waitresses in familiar roadside lonely petticoat upliftings

& especially secret gas-station solipisisms of johns, &
hometown alleys too,
who faded out in vast sordid movies, were shifted in dreams, woke
on a sudden Manhattan, and picked themselves up out of
basements hungover with heartless Tokay and horrors of
Third Avenue iron dreams & stumbled to unemployment
offices,
who walked all night with their shoes full of blood on the
snowbank docks waiting for a door in the East River to
open to a room full of steamheat and opium,
who created great suicidal dramas on the apartment cliff-banks of
the Hudson under the wartime blue floodlight of the moon
& their heads shall be crowned with laurel in oblivion,
who ate the lamb stew of the imagination or digested the crab at
the muddy bottom of the rivers of Bowery,
who wept at the romance of the streets with their pushcarts full of
onions and bad music,
who sat in boxes breathing in the darkness under the bridge, and
rose up to build harpsichords in their lofts,
who coughed on the sixth floor of Harlem crowned with flame
under the tubercular sky surrounded by orange crates of
theology,
who scribbled all night rocking and rolling over lofty incantations
which in the yellow morning where stanzas of gibberish,
who cooked rotten animals lung heart feet tail borsht & tortillas
dreaming of the pure vegetable kingdom,
who plunged themselves under meat trucks looking for an egg,
who threw their watches off the roof to cast their ballot for
Eternity outside of Time, & alarm clocks fell on their heads
every day for the next decade,
who cut their wrists three times successively unsuccessfully, gave up

and were forced to open antique stores where they thought
they were growing old and cried,

who were burned alive in their innocent flannel suits on Madison
Avenue amid blasts of leaden verse & the tanked-up clatter
of the iron regiments of fashion & the nitroglycerine shrieks
of the fairies of advertising & the mustard gas of sinister
intelligent editors, or were run down by the drunken
taxicabs of Absolute Reality,

who jumped off the Brooklyn Bridge this actually happened and
walked away unknown and forgotten into the ghostly daze
of Chinatown soup alleyways & firetrucks, not even one
free beer,

who sang out of their windows in despair, fell out of the subway
window, jumped in the filthy Passaic, leaped on negroes,
cried all over the street, danced on broken wineglasses
barefoot smashed phonograph records of nostalgic European
1930's German jazz finished the whiskey and threw up
groaning into the bloody toilet, moans in their ears and the
blast of colossal steamwhistles,

who barreled down the highways of the past journeying to each
other's hotrod-Golgotha jail-solitude watch or Birmingham
jazz incarnation,

who drove crosscountry seventytwo hours to find out if I had a
vision or you had a vision or he had a vision to find out
Eternity,

who journeyed to Denver, who died in Denver, who came back to
Denver & waited in vain, who watched over Denver &
brooded & loned in Denver and finally went away to find
out the Time, & now Denver is lonesome for her heroes,

who fell on their knees in hopeless cathedrals praying for each
other's salvation and light and breasts, until the soul
illuminated its hair for a second,

who crashed through their minds in jail waiting for impossible
criminals with golden heads and the charm of reality in
their hearts who sang sweet blues to Alcatraz,

who retired to Mexico to cultivate a habit, or Rocky Mount to
tender Buddha or Tangiers to boys or Southern Pacific to
the black locomotive or Harvard to Narcissus to Woodlawn
to the daisychain or grave,

who demanded sanity trials accusing the radio of hypnotism &
were left with their insanity & their hands & a hung jury,

who threw potato salad at CCNY lecturers on Dadaism and
subsequently presented themselves on the granite steps of
the madhouse with shaven heads and harlequin speech of
suicide, demanding instantaneous lobotomy,

and who were given instead the concrete void of insulin metrasol
electricity hydrotherapy psychotherapy occupational therapy
pingpong & amnesia,

who in humorless protest overturned only one symbolic pingpong
table, resting briefly in catatonia,

returning years later truly bald except for a wig of blood, and tears
and fingers, to the visible madman doom of the wards of
the madtowns of the East,

Pilgrim State's Rockland's and Greystone's foetid halls, bickering
with the echoes of the soul, rocking and rolling in the
midnight solitude-bench dolmen-realms of love, dream of life
a nightmare, bodies turned to stone as heavy as the moon,

with mother finally ******, and the last fantastic book flung out
of the tenement window, and the last door closed at 4 AM
and the last telephone slammed at the wall in reply and the
last furnished room emptied down to the last piece of
mental furniture, a yellow paper rose twisted on a wire
hanger in the closet, and even that imaginary, nothing but
a hopeful little bit of hallucination —

ah, Carl, while you are not safe I am not safe, and now you're
really in the total animal soup of time —
and who therefore ran through the icy streets obsessed with a
sudden flash of the alchemy of the use of the ellipse the
catalog the meter & the vibrating plane,
who dreamt and made incarnate gaps in Time & Space through
images juxtaposed, and trapped the archangel of the soul
between 2 visual images and joined the elemental verbs
and set the noun and dash of consciousness together jumping
with sensation of Pater Omnipotens Aeterna Deus
to recreate the syntax and measure of poor human prose and stand
before you speechless and intelligent and shaking with
shame, rejected yet confessing out the soul to conform to
the rhythm of thought in his naked and endless head,
the madman bum and angel beat in Time, unknown, yet putting
down here what might be left to say in time come after
death,
and rose reincarnate in the ghostly clothes of jazz in the goldhorn
shadow of the band and blew the suffering of America's
naked mind for love into an eli eli lamma lamma sabacthani
saxophone cry that shivered the cities down to the last radio
with the absolute heart of the poem of life butchered out of their
own bodies good to eat a thousand years.

II

What sphinx of cement and aluminum bashed open their skulls
and ate up their brains and imagination?
Moloch! Solitude! Filth! Ugliness! Ashcans and unobtainable
dollars! Children screaming under the stairways! Boys
sobbing in armies! Old men weeping in the parks!
Moloch! Moloch! Nightmare of Moloch! Moloch the loveless!
Mental Moloch! Moloch the heavy judger of men!
Moloch the incomprehensible prison! Moloch the crossbone
soulless jailhouse and Congress of sorrows! Moloch whose
buildings are judgement! Moloch the vast stone of war!
Moloch the stunned governments!
Moloch whose mind is pure machinery! Moloch whose blood is
running money! Moloch whose fingers are ten armies!
Moloch whose breast is a cannibal dynamo! Moloch whose
ear is a smoking tomb!
Moloch whose eyes are a thousand blind windows! Moloch whose
skyscrapers stand in the long streets like endless Jehovahs!
Moloch whose factories dream and croak in the fog!
Moloch whose smokestacks and antennae crown the cities!
Moloch whose love is endless oil and stone! Moloch whose soul is
electricity and banks! Moloch whose poverty is the
specter of genius! Moloch whose fate is a cloud of sexless
hydrogen! Moloch whose name is the Mind!
Moloch in whom I sit lonely! Moloch in whom I dream Angels!
Crazy in Moloch! C...sucker in Moloch! Lacklove and
manless in Moloch!
Moloch who entered my soul early! Moloch in whom I am a
consciousness without a body! Moloch who frightened me
out of my natural ecstasy! Moloch whom I abandon!
Wake up in Moloch! Light streaming out of the sky!

Moloch! Moloch! Robot apartments! invisible suburbs!
   skeleton treasuries! blind capitals! demonic industries!
   spectral nations! invincible madhouses! granite cocks!
   monstrous bombs!
They broke their backs lifting Moloch to Heaven! Pavements,
   trees, radios, tons! lifting the city to Heaven which exists
   and is everywhere about us!
Visions! omens! hallucinations! miracles! ecstasies! gone down
   the American river!
Dreams! adorations! illuminations! religions! the whole
   boatload of sensitive bullshit!
Breakthroughs! over the river! flips and crucifixions! gone down
   the flood! Highs! Epiphanies! Despairs! Ten years'
   animal screams and suicides! Minds! New loves! Mad
   generation! down on the rocks of Time!
Real holy laughter in the river! They saw it all! the wild eyes!
   the holy yells! They bade farewell! They jumped off the
   roof! to solitude! waving! carrying flowers! Down to
   the river! into the street!

III

Carl Solomon! I'm with you in Rockland
    where you're madder than I am
I'm with you in Rockland
    where you must feel very strange
I'm with you in Rockland
    where you imitate the shade of my mother
I'm with you in Rockland
    where you've murdered your twelve secretaries
I'm with you in Rockland
    where you laugh at this invisible humor
I'm with you in Rockland
    where we are great writers on the same dreadful typewriter
I'm with you in Rockland
    where your condition has become serious and is reported on
    the radio
I'm with you in Rockland
    where the faculties of the skull no longer admit the worms
    of the senses
I'm with you in Rockland
    where you drink the tea of the breasts of the spinsters of
    Utica
I'm with you in Rockland
    where you pun on the bodies of your nurses the harpies of
    the Bronx
I'm with you in Rockland
    where you scream in a straightjacket that you're losing the
    game of the actual pingpong of the abyss
I'm with you in Rockland
    where you bang on the catatonic piano the soul is innocent
    and immortal it should never die ungodly in an armed
    madhouse

20

I'm with you in Rockland
>where fifty more shocks will never return your soul to its
body again from its pilgrimage to a cross in the void
I'm with you in Rockland
>where you accuse your doctors of insanity and plot the
Hebrew socialist revolution against the fascist national
Golgotha
I'm with you in Rockland
>where you will split the heavens of Long Island and resurrect
your living human Jesus from the superhuman tomb
I'm with you in Rockland
>where there are twentyfive-thousand mad comrades all
together singing the final stanzas of the Internationale
I'm with you in Rockland
>where we hug and kiss the United States under our
bedsheets   the United States that coughs all night and won't
let us sleep
I'm with you in Rockland
>where we wake up electrified out of the coma by our own
souls' airplanes roaring over the roof they've come to drop
angelic bombs the hospital illuminates itself   imaginary
walls collapse   O skinny legions run outside   O starry-
spangled shock of mercy the eternal war is here   O victory
forget your underwear we're free
I'm with you in Rockland
>in my dreams you walk dripping from a sea-journey on the
highway across America in tears to the door of my cottage
in the Western night

San Francisco   1955-56

FOOTNOTE TO HOWL

Holy! Holy! Holy! Holy! Holy! Holy! Holy! Holy! Holy!
   Holy! Holy! Holy! Holy! Holy! Holy!
The world is holy! The soul is holy! The skin is holy! The nose
   is holy! The tongue and cock and hand and asshole holy!
Everything is holy! everybody's holy! everywhere is holy!
   everyday is in eternity! Everyman's an angel!
The bum's as holy as the seraphim! the madman is holy as you my
   soul are holy!
The typewriter is holy the poem is holy the voice is holy the
   hearers are holy the ecstasy is holy!
Holy Peter holy Allen holy Solomon holy Lucien holy Kerouac
   holy Huncke holy Burroughs holy Cassady holy the unknown
   buggered and suffering beggars holy the hideous human
   angels!
Holy my mother in the insane asylum! Holy the cocks of the
   grandfathers of Kansas!
Holy the groaning saxophone! Holy the bop apocalypse! Holy the
   jazzbands marijuana hipsters peace & junk & drums!
Holy the solitudes of skyscrapers and pavements! Holy the
   cafeterias filled with the millions! Holy the mysterious
   rivers of tears under the streets!
Holy the lone juggernaut! Holy the vast lamb of the middle-
   class! Holy the crazy shepherds of rebellion! Who digs
   Los Angeles IS Los Angeles!
Holy New York Holy San Francisco Holy Peoria & Seattle Holy
   Paris Holy Tangiers Holy Moscow Holy Istanbul!
Holy time in eternity holy eternity in time holy the clocks in space
   holy the fourth dimension holy the fifth International holy
   the Angel in Moloch!

22

Holy the sea holy the desert holy the railroad holy the locomotive
holy the visions holy the hallucinations holy the miracles
holy the eyeball holy the abyss!
Holy forgiveness! mercy! charity! faith! Holy! Ours! bodies!
suffering! magnanimity!
Holy the supernatural extra brilliant intelligent kindness of the
soul!

A SUPERMARKET IN CALIFORNIA

What thoughts I have of you tonight, Walt Whitman, for I walked down the sidestreets under the trees with a headache self-conscious looking at the full moon.

In my hungry fatigue, and shopping for images, I went into the neon fruit supermarket, dreaming of your enumerations!

What peaches and what penumbras! Whole families shopping at night! Aisles full of husbands! Wives in the avocados, babies in the tomatoes! — and you, Garcia Lorca, what were you doing down by the watermelons?

I saw you, Walt Whitman, childless, lonely old grubber, poking among the meats in the refrigerator and eyeing the grocery boys.

I heard you asking questions of each: Who killed the pork chops? What price bananas? Are you my Angel?

I wandered in and out of the brilliant stacks of cans following you, and followed in my imagination by the store detective.

We strode down the open corridors together in our solitary fancy tasting artichokes, possessing every frozen delicacy, and never passing the cashier.

Where are we going, Walt Whitman? The doors close in an hour. Which way does your beard point tonight?

(I touch your book and dream of our odyssey in the supermarket and feel absurd.)

Will we walk all night through solitary streets? The trees add shade to shade, lights out in the houses, we'll both be lonely.

Will we stroll dreaming of the lost America of love past
blue automobiles in driveways, home to our silent cottage?
Ah, dear father, graybeard, lonely old courage-teacher,
what America did you have when Charon quit poling his ferry
and you got out on a smoking bank and stood watching the
boat disappear on the black waters of Lethe?

Berkeley 1955

TRANSCRIPTION OF ORGAN MUSIC

The flower in the glass peanut bottle formerly in the kitchen
    crooked to take a place in the light,
the closet door opened, because I used it before, it kindly stayed
    open waiting for me, its owner.

I began to feel my misery in pallet on floor, listening to music,
    my misery, that's why I want to sing.
The room closed down on me, I expected the presence of the
    Creator, I saw my gray painted walls and ceiling, they
    contained my room, they contained me
as the sky contained my garden,
I opened my door
    The rambler vine climbed up the cottage post, the
leaves in the night still where the day had placed them, the animal
heads of the flowers where they had arisen
    to think at the sun

    Can I bring back the words? Will thought of transcription
haze my mental open eye?

    The kindly search for growth, the gracious desire to exist of
the flowers, my near ecstasy at existing among them
    The privilege to witness my existence — you too must seek
the sun . . .

    My books piled up before me for my use
    waiting in space where I placed them, they haven't
disappeared, time's left its remnants and qualities for me to use —
my words piled up, my texts, my manuscripts, my loves.

I had a moment of clarity, saw the feeling in the heart of things, walked out to the garden crying.

Saw the red blossoms in the night light, sun's gone, they had all grown, in a moment, and were waiting stopped in time for the day sun to come and give them. . . .

Flowers which as in a dream at sunset I watered faithfully not knowing how much I loved them.

I am so lonely in my glory — except they too out there — I looked up — those red bush blossoms beckoning and peering in the window waiting in blind love, their leaves too have hope and are upturned top flat to the sky to receive — all creation open to receive — the flat earth itself.

The music descends, as does the tall bending stalk of the heavy blossom, because it has to, to stay alive, to continue to the last drop of joy.

The world knows the love that's in its breast as in the flower, the suffering lonely world.

The Father is merciful.

The light socket is crudely attached to the ceiling, after the house was built, to receive a plug which sticks in it alright, and serves my phonograph now . . .

The closet door is open for me, where I left it, since I left it open, it has graciously stayed open.

The kitchen has no door, the hole there will admit me should I wish to enter the kitchen.

I remember when I first got laid, H.P. graciously took my cherry, I sat on the docks of Provincetown, age 23, joyful, elevated in hope with the Father, the door to the womb was open to admit me if I wished to enter.

There are unused electricity plugs all over my house if I ever need them.

The kitchen window is open, to admit air . . .

The telephone — sad to relate — sits on the floor — I haven't the money to get it connected —

I want people to bow as they see me and say he is gifted with poetry, he has seen the presence of the Creator.

And the Creator gave me a shot of his presence to gratify my wish, so as not to cheat me of my yearning for him.

Berkeley 1955

SUNFLOWER SUTRA

I walked on the banks of the tincan banana dock and sat down
under the huge shade of a Southern Pacific locomotive to
look at the sunset over the box house hills and cry.
Jack Kerouac sat beside me on a busted rusty iron pole,
companion, we thought the same thoughts of the soul,
bleak and blue and sad-eyed, surrounded by the gnarled
steel roots of trees of machinery.
The oily water on the river mirrored the red sky, sun sank on top
of final Frisco peaks, no fish in that stream, no hermit in
those mounts, just ourselves rheumy-eyed and hungover
like old bums on the riverbank, tired and wily.
Look at the Sunflower, he said, there was a dead gray shadow
against the sky, big as a man, sitting dry on top of a pile of
ancient sawdust —
— I rushed up enchanted — it was my first sunflower, memories
of Blake — my visions — Harlem
and Hells of the Eastern rivers, bridges clanking Joes Greasy
Sandwiches, dead baby carriages, black treadless tires
forgotten and unretreaded, the poem of the riverbank,
condoms & pots, steel knives, nothing stainless, only the
dank muck and the razor sharp artifacts passing into the
past —
and the gray Sunflower poised against the sunset, crackly bleak
and dusty with the smut and smog and smoke of olden
locomotives in its eye —
corolla of bleary spikes pushed down and broken like a battered
crown, seeds fallen out of its face, soon-to-be-toothless
mouth of sunny air, sunrays obliterated on its hairy head
like a dried wire spiderweb,
leaves stuck out like arms out of the stem, gestures from the

sawdust root, broke pieces of plaster fallen out of the black twigs, a dead fly in its ear,

Unholy battered old thing you were, my sunflower O my soul, I loved you then!

The grime was no man's grime but death and human locomotives,

all that dress of dust, that veil of darkened railroad skin, that smog of cheek, that eyelid of black mis'ry, that sooty hand or phallus or protuberance of artificial worse-than-dirt — industrial — modern — all that civilization spotting your crazy golden crown —

and those blear thoughts of death and dusty loveless eyes and ends and withered roots below, in the home-pile of sand and sawdust, rubber dollar bills, skin of machinery, the guts and innards of the weeping coughing car, the empty lonely tincans with their rusty tongues alack, what more could I name, the smoked ashes of some cock cigar, the c . . . s of wheelbarrows and the milky breasts of cars, wornout asses out of chairs & sphincters of dynamos — all these

entangled in your mummied roots — and you there standing before me in the sunset, all your glory in your form!

A perfect beauty of a sunflower! a perfect excellent lovely sunflower existence! a sweet natural eye to the new hip moon, woke up alive and excited grasping in the sunset shadow sunrise golden monthly breeze!

How many flies buzzed round you innocent of your grime, while you cursed the heavens of the railroad and your flower soul?

Poor dead flower? when did you forget you were a flower? when did you look at your skin and decide you were an impotent dirty old locomotive? the ghost of a locomotive? the specter and shade of a once powerful mad American locomotive?

30

You were never no locomotive, Sunflower, you were a sunflower!

And you Locomotive, you are a locomotive, forget me not!

So I grabbed up the skeleton thick sunflower and stuck it at my
    side like a scepter,

and deliver my sermon to my soul, and Jack's soul too, and anyone
    who'll listen,

— We're not our skin of grime, we're not our dread bleak dusty
    imageless locomotive, we're all beautiful golden sunflowers
    inside, we're blessed by our own seed & golden hairy naked
    accomplishment-bodies growing into mad black formal sun-
    flowers in the sunset, spied on by our eyes under the shadow
    of the mad locomotive riverbank sunset Frisco hilly tincan
    evening sitdown vision.

Berkeley 1955

AMERICA

America I've given you all and now I'm nothing.
America two dollars and twentyseven cents January 17, 1956.
I can't stand on my own mind.
America when will we end the human war?
Go fuck yourself with your atom bomb.
I don't feel good don't bother me.
I won't write my poem till I'm in my right mind.
America when will you be angelic?
When will you take off your clothes?
When will you look at yourself through the grave?
When will you be worthy of your million Trotskyites?
America why are your libraries full of tears?
America when will you send your eggs to India?
I'm sick of your insane demands.
When can I go into the supermarket and buy what I need with my
    good looks?
America after all it is you and I who are perfect not the next world.
Your machinery is too much for me.
You made me want to be a saint.
There must be some other way to settle this argument.
Burroughs is in Tangiers I don't think he'll come back it's sinister.
Are you being sinister or is this some form of practical joke?
I'm trying to come to the point.
I refuse to give up my obsession.
America stop pushing I know what I'm doing.
America the plum blossoms are falling.
I haven't read the newspapers for months, everyday somebody goes
    on trial for murder.
America I feel sentimental about the Wobblies.
America I used to be a communist when I was a kid I'm not sorry.

I smoke marijuana every chance I get.
I sit in my house for days on end and stare at the roses in the closet.
When I go to Chinatown I get drunk and never get laid.
My mind is made up there's going to be trouble.
You should have seen me reading Marx.
My psychoanalyst thinks I'm perfectly right.
I won't say the Lord's Prayer.
I have mystical visions and cosmic vibrations.
America I still haven't told you what you did to Uncle Max after
        he came over from Russia.

I'm addressing you.
Are you going to let your emotional life be run by Time Magazine?
I'm obsessed by Time Magazine.
I read it every week.
Its cover stares at me every time I slink past the corner candystore.
I read it in the basement of the Berkeley Public Library.
It's always telling me about responsibility. Businessmen are serious.
        Movie producers are serious. Everybody's serious but me.
It occurs to me that I am America.
I am talking to myself again.

Asia is rising against me.
I haven't got a chinaman's chance.
I'd better consider my national resources.
My national resources consist of two joints of marijuana millions of
        genitals an unpublishable private literature that goes 1400
        miles an hour and twentyfive-thousand mental institutions.
I say nothing about my prisons nor the millions of underprivileged
        who live in my flowerpots under the light of five hundred
        suns.

I have abolished the whorehouses of France, Tangiers is the next
     to go.
My ambition is to be President despite the fact that I'm a Catholic.

America how can I write a holy litany in your silly mood?
I will continue like Henry Ford my strophes are as individual as
     his automobiles more so they're all different sexes.
America I will sell you strophes $2500 apiece $500 down on your
     old strophe
America free Tom Mooney
America save the Spanish Loyalists
America Sacco & Vanzetti must not die
America I am the Scottsboro boys.
America when I was seven momma took me to Communist Cell
     meetings   they sold us garbanzos a handful per ticket
     a ticket costs a nickel and the speeches were free
     everybody was angelic and sentimental about the workers
     it was all so sincere you have no idea what a good thing
     the party was in 1835 Scott Nearing was a grand old man
     a real mensch Mother Bloor made me cry I once saw
     Israel Amter plain. Everybody must have been a spy.
America you don't really want to go to war.
America it's them bad Russians.
Them Russians them Russians and them Chinamen. And them
     Russians.
The Russia wants to eat us alive. The Russia's power mad. She
     wants to take our cars from out our garages.
Her wants to grab Chicago. Her needs a Red Readers' Digest.
     Her wants our auto plants in Siberia. Him big bureaucracy
     running our fillingstations.

34

That no good. Ugh. Him make Indians learn read. Him need
    big black niggers. Hah. Her make us all work sixteen hours
    a day. Help.
America this is quite serious.
America this is the impression I get from looking in the television
    set.
America is this correct?
I'd better get right down to the job.
It's true I don't want to join the Army or turn lathes in precision
    parts factories, I'm nearsighted and psychopathic anyway.
America I'm putting my queer shoulder to the wheel.

IN THE BAGGAGE ROOM AT GREYHOUND

I

In the depths of the Greyhound Terminal
sitting dumbly on a baggage truck looking at the sky waiting for
      the Los Angeles Express to depart
worrying about eternity over the Post Office roof in the night-time
      red downtown heaven,
staring through my eyeglasses I realized shuddering these thoughts
      were not eternity, nor the poverty of our lives, irritable
      baggage clerks,
nor the millions of weeping relatives surrounding the buses waving
      goodbye,
nor other millions of the poor rushing around from city to city to
      see their loved ones,
nor an indian dead with fright talking to a huge cop by the Coke
      machine,
nor this trembling old lady with a cane taking the last trip of her
      life,
nor the red capped cynical porter collecting his quarters and
      smiling over the smashed baggage,
nor me looking around at the horrible dream,
nor mustached negro Operating Clerk named Spade, dealing out
      with his marvelous long hand the fate of thousands of
      express packages,
nor fairy Sam in the basement limping from leaden trunk to trunk,
nor Joe at the counter with his nervous breakdown smiling cowardly
      at the customers,
nor the grayish-green whale's stomach interior loft where we keep
      the baggage in hideous racks,

hundreds of suitcases full of tragedy rocking back and forth waiting
       to be opened,
nor the baggage that's lost, nor damaged handles, nameplates
       vanished, busted wires & broken ropes, whole trunks
       exploding on the concrete floor,
nor seabags emptied into the night in the final warehouse.

II

Yet Spade reminded me of Angel, unloading a bus,
dressed in blue overalls black face official Angel's workman cap,
pushing with his belly a huge tin horse piled high with black
       baggage,
looking up as he passed the yellow light bulb of the loft
and holding high on his arm an iron shepherd's crook.

III

It was the racks, I realized, sitting myself on top of them now as is
       my wont at lunchtime to rest my tired foot,
it was the racks, great wooden shelves and stanchions posts and
       beams assembled floor to roof jumbled with baggage,
— the Japanese white metal postwar trunk gaudily flowered &
       headed for Fort Bragg,
one Mexican green paper package in purple rope adorned with
       names for Nogales,
hundreds of radiators all at once for Eureka,
crates of Hawaiian underwear,
rolls of posters scattered over the Peninsula, nuts to Sacramento,
one human eye for Napa,

an aluminum box of human blood for Stockton
and a little red package of teeth for Calistoga —
it was the racks and these on the racks I saw naked in electric
       light the night before I quit,
the racks were created to hang our possessions, to keep us together,
       a temporary shift in space,
God's only way of building the rickety structure of Time,
to hold the bags to send on the roads, to carry our luggage from
       place to place
looking for a bus to ride us back home to Eternity where the heart
       was left and farewell tears began.

IV

A swarm of baggage sitting by the counter as the transcontinental
       bus pulls in.
The clock registering 12.15 A.M., May 9, 1956, the second hand
       moving forward, red.
Getting ready to load my last bus. — Farewell, Walnut Creek
       Richmond Vallejo Portland Pacific Highway
Fleet-footed Quicksilver, God of transience.
One last package sits lone at midnight sticking up out of the Coast
       rack high as the dusty fluorescent light.

The wage they pay us is too low to live on. Tragedy reduced to
       numbers.
This for the poor shepherds. I am a communist.

Farewell ye Greyhound where I suffered so much,
hurt my knee and scraped my hand and built my pectoral muscles
       big as vagina.

AN ASPHODEL

O dear sweet rosy
        unattainable desire
. . . how sad, no way
        to change the mad
cultivated asphodel, the
        visible reality . . .

and skin's appalling
        petals — how inspired
to be so lying in the living
        room drunk naked
and dreaming, in the absence
        of electricity . . .
over and over eating the low root
        of the asphodel,
gray fate . . .

        rolling in generation
on the flowery couch
        as on a bank in Arden —
my only rose tonite's the treat
        of my own nudity.

SONG

The weight of the world
       is love.
Under the burden
       of solitude,
under the burden
       of dissatisfaction

       the weight,
the weight we carry
       is love.

Who can deny?
       In dreams
it touches
       the body,
in thought
       constructs
a miracle,
       in imagination
anguishes
       till born
in human —

looks out of the heart
       burning with purity —
for the burden of life
       is love,

but we carry the weight
       wearily,

and so must rest
in the arms of love
    at last,
must rest in the arms
    of love.

No rest
    without love,
no sleep
    without dreams
of love —
    be mad or chill
obsessed with angels
    or machines,
the final wish
    is love
— cannot be bitter,
    cannot deny,
cannot withhold
    if denied :

the weight is too heavy

    — must give
for no return
    as thought
is given
    in solitude
in all the excellence
    of its excess.

The warm bodies
      shine together
in the darkness,
      the hand moves
to the center
      of the flesh,
the skin trembles
      in happiness
and the soul comes
      joyful to the eye —

yes, yes,
      that's what
I wanted,
      I always wanted,
I always wanted,
      to return
to the body
      where I was born.

WILD ORPHAN

Blandly mother
takes him strolling
    by railroad and by river
— he's the son of the absconded
    hot rod angel —
and he imagines cars
    and rides them in his dreams,

so lonely growing up among
    the imaginary automobiles
and dead souls of Tarrytown

    to create
out of his own imagination
    the beauty of his wild
forebears — a mythology
    he cannot inherit.

Will he later hallucinate
    his gods? Waking
among mysteries with
    an insane gleam
of recollection?

    The recognition —
something so rare
    in his soul,
met only in dreams
    — nostalgias
of another life.

A question of the soul.
      And the injured
losing their injury
      in their innocence
— a cock, a cross,
      an excellence of love.

And the father grieves
      in flophouse
complexities of memory
      a thousand miles
away, unknowing
      of the unexpected
youthful stranger
      bumming toward his door.

In back of the real

railroad yard in San Jose
      I wandered desolate
in front of a tank factory
      and sat on a bench
near the switchman's shack.

A flower lay on the hay on
      the asphalt highway
— the dread hay flower
      I thought — It had a
brittle black stem and
      corolla of yellowish dirty
spikes like Jesus' inchlong
      crown, and a soiled
dry center cotton tuft
      like a used shaving brush
that's been lying under
      the garage for a year.

Yellow, yellow flower, and
      flower of industry,
tough spikey ugly flower,
      flower nonetheless,
with the form of the great yellow
      Rose in your brain!
This is the flower of the World.

Printed in the USA
CPSIA information can be obtained
at www.ICGtesting.com
LVHW040548221223
767136LV00002B/294